JACK AND THE BEANCOUNTERS

A 21ST CENTURY FABLE OF FINANCIAL ENGINEERING, SKULLDUGGERY - AND SALVATION BROUGHT ABOUT BY SELF HELP, TOLERANCE AND CANNY MARKETING

BY PETER N YOUNG

This book is dedicated to Dianne and Nicola without whose help it would not have been conceived, and without whom it would certainly never have been completed.

INTRODUCTION

The Oxford English Dictionary defines a fable as "A short story, especially one in which animals are the characters, which conveys a moral".

Wikipedia says that one who writes a fable is a "fabulist" and numbers among the classical fabulists a string of distinguished storytellers from Aesop to Hans Christian Anderson.

We have no aspiration to join the Wikipedia "fabulist list". But the story can claim to be a fable.

Created over one Christmas vacation period, with the invaluable help of the wife and daughter, it is certainly short – requiring some padding to reach the requisite minimum 24 pages for self publication under the Amazon Create Space banner.

It also features animals.

All of them are human, which some might say excludes the story from the fable stable.

But, like it or not, we are animals too. Indeed there is a fine Spanish saying that the human animal is the only animal which trips over the same stone twice (this saying seems to have found its way into many languages in one version or another). The particular stones portrayed in this fable have undoubtedly been tripped over many times before in the history of the human race and surely will trip us again.

And the story certainly sets out to convey a moral.

In the early 21st Century, what moral is there of greater relevance than the moral conveyed by the fable of Jack and the Bean Counters?

Unfettered greed, misdirected creativity and the sheer gullibility of a tolerant middle class have led us Westerners into a dark place from which we yet have to see an exit. Our capacity to make and sell things that people might want to buy has largely gone, perhaps forever. Our banks are broke, as are most of their customers. And the will to get up and go – to build a better world with our bare hands – is almost a lost memory.

We probably don't know how to find our way out of the mess we have allowed to be created. And, if we were to rush to acquire the knowledge, we have sunk into a pit of apathy so deep we may not even have the will to seek the exit.

"Someone will save us. They always have. Just don't ask me to. Something will turn up" say millions of 21st Century Micawbers as they go myopically about their business.

Jack was myopic. Hard working and honest, but gullible (and perhaps a bit greedy?). Easy pickings were dangled and Jack, as so many of us have done, fell.

When faced with the dire consequences of his folly, he was paralysed into inaction. Only his fine and worldly wife came to the rescue – was is not ever so?

Of course the writer projects his or her prejudices onto any narrative. How can we do other?

And my prejudice is the salvational power of Marketing.

Marketing is not an easy concept to tie down. In the early 21st century The Henley Management College brought together a group of distinguished scholars to revisit the thorny topic of Marketing Definitions. They studied some 100 extant definitions and concluded among other things that greater clarity and precision should be brought to future definitions.

But no consensus emerged as to which definition of Marketing should rule. The ship sailed on without a compass (or with hundreds of conflicting compasses, which is even more confusing. At least with no compass at all you can fall back on experience and common sense).

To guide Jack and his inventive (dare I say Innovative) wife the definition which showed the way was the most basic of definitions of Marketing - "satisfying or anticipating consumer needs (or wants) profitably".

I have my own definition of what marketing is all about – or should be – cobbled together for a series of college lectures pretentiously entitled "An Introduction to Marketing".

The definition is a touch long, but quite complete, and very practical. It is not so much about marketing theory but it is very much about marketing practice. I reproduce it here in full for your consideration.

- *The marketer initiates the process of identifying potential customer wants and needs as they pertain to an actual or potential offering of his organisation.*

- *The marketer ensures that his or her offering is perceived by the target as fulfilling those wants or needs better than any competing offer, and thereby secures a voluntary exchange of values to the mutual benefit of the target and offerer.*

- *The marketer's primary function is to secure an exchange – in the case of Commerce a "Sale" or "Purchase".*

If Jack's magnificent wife didn't do just, that what did she do?

And if she had not done it, where would Jack be today? Where would his family be?

And what might have become of his neighbours and the village community of which they were part and to which they made such a valuable contribution?

The final moral of the tale?

I remain optimistic. There is something of Jack's wife in all of us.

The concealed but adept marketer

As Michelangelo with his sculptor's chisel set free the statue hidden in the stone, we just have to let the marketer out.

Duxford
Cambridge
October 2013

JACK AND THE BEANCOUNTERS

A 21ST CENTURY FABLE

PART I - DESCENT INTO DARKNESS

AGE OF INNOCENCE

Once upon a time - indeed quite recently - there was a farmer who lived in a comfortable but modest home on the edge of a village with his lovely wife (once a cheerleader, class valedictorian, homecoming queen, model and page 3 girl, but now devoted wife and mother) and their two young children.

Jack grew and farmed coffee.

His smallholding was of modest size. He grew coffee to drink, to sell and to barter for food with his neighbours. They too were farmers.

On one side Joe farmed corn. On the other side James had a dairy and livestock for meat, milk and leather. And Annabelle grew vegetables.

The rest of Jack's coffee beans were sold to the good people of the nearby village. His most loyal customer was the Mayor. Jack also supplied Starbucks.

INVASION OF THE SUITS

One glorious fall morning Jack stood admiring a whole hill of beans. He had just brought in his best ever harvest.

In his hand was the small, battered diary left to him in his father's will.

The old man's last words to Jack had been:

"All I can give you now, son, is good advice".

"Open the diary on page one when the good times come."

"Open her up on page two when the bad times come around."

Sitting in his dad's solid old carved rocking chair on the weather beaten porch of his modest but comfortable home Jack reflected on the record harvest. He reckoned that now was just the time to open up the diary for his dad's first slice of homespun advice.

He let his eyes rest on the opened page of the diary and digested the wisdom of that loving old man, who had cared for him from cradle to his own grave, barely noticing the small dust cloud that appeared in the distance and moved slowly up the dirt driveway towards the farm.

"Invest for the future when the times are good" said the diary.

"Invest for the future?" pondered Jack.

"Well, the times are sure good right now." thought Jack. "But how? Investments? Never been there before. Sounds complicated. Sounds risky too."

But the thought had barely entered his head when the dust cloud resolved itself into a sleek, shining bus – a bit like the Greyhound bus you can still see in the old movies on cable.

The bus was towing an enormous trailer and the effect of the whole caravan was something like a cabin cruiser towing a barn.

Up rolled the bus, up rolled the tow-load and out jumped a smart looking bespectacled young man in a dark suit.

"You have to be Jack!" he said. "And that has got to be the biggest hill of beans I ever saw."

"Too right, son" said Jack. "And I was just figuring out what to do with that hill and when."

"We" said the Suit, waiving his arm at the bus and the barn-on-wheels "are the folk you need to help you. And now is just the right time"

"We, Jack, are Bean Counters".

"But we are much, much more than that. We are financial service providers. We are investment counsellors. We are exactly what you need right now and you will be reassured that we will be at your side for the rest of your life."

Jack reckoned that sounded pretty encouraging and resolved to listen further.

"First" said the Suit "we count your beans. Then we hand over to you all the beans you need this year to drink fine coffee, barter with your neighbours for food, sell to the village and supply Starbucks."

"The rest of your beans will be loaded into our trailer. That, Jack is your investment."

"After a year we will give you back a whole lot of beans – never less than 15% of all the beans you give us. Maybe more. We call those dividend beans."

"Probably that's enough for you to drink, barter and sell in a year. You may choose never to work again. You may sell the farm – we can arrange that. You have worked hard. You deserve a rest. Go on a cruise or fifty. Divorce the wife and get a new cheerleader."

"But if you are determined to go on working as before, skip the cruises, work your fingers to the bone and stay with the old gal…" (he could not at that moment see Jack's gorgeous and youthful wife, a veritable eyeful of arm candy who would make a run of the mill trophy wife look drab by comparison, or he would never have made this disparaging remark) "…that's fine too".

"Give us your surplus beans every year and we will give you a minimum dividend of 15% of all the beans you ever entrust to us until you drop dead of well earned exhaustion."

"And this, Jack is the greatest miracle of all. You or your heirs can have all the beans back you invested with us at any time. And we guarantee there will be more beans than you put into the trailer."

"We will tell you every working day exactly how many beans you have with us – we will publish the figures in the Financial Times and the Wall Street Journal. Detailed information will be available in real time on the Internet."

"But if that doesn't reassure, you can come into the trailer at any time and check on your beans. They will be right there for all of you to see."

"Now how does that sound Jack? How does that sound?"

Well, it sounded pretty good to Jack. And after a brief family consultation there ensued a lot of hand shaking and signing of contracts.

The grin had barely passed from the smooth, unlined face of the visitor when the bus and the trailer disgorged a veritable army of Suits who set too with a will.

In no time the beans were counted.

As the First Suit handed over Jack's "12 month working beans" in neatly labelled sacks, a thought occurred to Jack.

"May I ask what is in this for you, Sir? I do not want to pry, but it seems that there must be something that makes this worthwhile for you and all your fellow be-suited bean counters?"

"True indeed Jack" said First Suit. "We do this because we love the work, of course. And we grease the wheels of commerce. We make people like you and the villagers, who work your fields for pay, happier humans beings – or if I may jest a moment – happier "human beans"._

He gave a dry chuckle.

"But yes Jack, we do take an honest and modest remuneration for our services. We expect to take maybe 20% of all the beans for ourselves each year. If things go well of course. If not, perhaps a bit less"

Jack pondered this a moment and persisted (unusually, for persistence was not his forte).

"You give me at least 15% of my beans at the end of each year and you take 20% for yourselves. And the pile of beans in the trailer grows each year. You guys must be magicians." he said.

"Not magicians, Jack. Just creative engineers!" the Suit chuckled with reassuringly twinkling eyes.

"I tell you what, Jack. When we come back next year to hand over your annual bean dividend, I will lift up the lid and show you just a little bit of our operation."

And with a reassuring waive of his elegant hand the Suit and his fellow bean counters departed.

END YEAR I – DIVIDEND TIME

A year passed quickly as it does on a coffee bean farm. And it seemed just like yesterday that the Suits had sped down the road when once again the cloud of dust resolved itself into the rolling dream factory as it raced up the driveway to the house.

In no time at all the fresh, new hill of beans was counted, the bulk of it loaded into the trailer, and Jack stood admiring the smart sacks of coffee left standing by the house for his own use.

Of course there were more sacks by the house than last year – about double and it occurred to Jack that he now had a storage problem.

But why so much coffee for his own use? Why almost double last year?

Of course. He had forgotten. The annual dividend on the beans he invested last year was due and had been added to a new year of working beans.

When he mentioned the storage problem to the helpful Suit who was exhaustedly mopping his brow after the heavy responsibility of bullying his colleagues into frantic counting, the Suit naturally had a solution.

"Of course, Jack, of course. You have here in front of you your annual working beans and the dividend of the profits from the beans you gave us last year. It is probably more than you need for a year. Why not reinvest the dividend beans with us. More beans invested, more dividend next year. And no storage problems!"

It seemed a pretty good idea to Jack, more hands were shaken and more beans loaded into the trailer.

As the Suit at last turned away to depart for another year a couple of thoughts came into Jack's mind.

First, the Suit had promised a year back to share a bit of his magic with Jack.

And secondly Jack hadn't actually seen anything of the beans from last year (of which the Internet assured him there were now twice as many as there were at the beginning of the year). The dividend beans had been paid out of this year's harvest – the new hill of beans. Jack wondered how his old beans were getting on and what miracle was turning one hundred beans into two hundred each year.

"Of course. Of course. Come into the trailer" said the Suit. "It's pretty complicated, and I don't really understand it myself – I leave that to the techies. But I am sure you will be enlightened and much reassured."

THE DREAM FACTORY

So Jack climbed up the ramp into the giant trailer.

The inside seemed even more cavernous than the outside had led him to expect.

Down the centre of the warehouse was a row of huge glass sided tanks. But because the glass was opaque all that could be seen from outside the tanks were the vague shapes of small spherical objects crowding against the sides, further obscured by what seemed to be dark grains of a substance, which also could not be clearly identified. It was impossible to see into the tanks, which were several feet taller than Jack, even when he stood on tiptoe.

Around the tanks were arrayed worktables covered with tools such as saws, pliers, vices, cutters, wrenches, glue pots and paintbrushes. At each worktable sat a Suit busily wielding the various tools in a veritable sea of beans.

"What…" said Jack "are these guys doing?"

"They are the wizards" said the Suit. "They are the techies. They are the best. They used to work for the Pentagon during the cold war. Top brains. And now the cold war is over they have no job, no challenge. So we put them to work growing your bean stock."

"They do it for other farmers too, you know. And they grow their corn stock, their meat yield, their vegetables – all. Nothing they can't do."

It all looked very confusing to Jack.

One Suit was cutting beans in half. Another was painting whole beans and another painting part beans. Yet another was sticking bits of bean together.

Several Suits were throwing beans up in the air and watching how they fell. Others were throwing beans, half beans and bean fragments at each other."

In one corner a Suit seemed to be sticking half a bean to a crushed ear of corn. And what looked worryingly like a cow's udder was being wrapped around a giant sphere of what appeared to be ground, reconstituted coffee.

Every now and again a "finished" object was hurled into an empty tank.

And everywhere were what appeared to be auditors with large pocket calculators tapping screens.

"They are the monitors" whispered First Suit. "They check the stock and allocate inventory value".

Jack felt very humble and very bemused. But the atmosphere was so intense and the operators and monitors were so well dressed that he felt it churlish to seem un-enlightened and un-reassured as he beat a hasty retreat back down the ramp to the sanity of his home.

"I leave it all in your competent hands" he said determinedly. "See you next year".

And so he did.

YEARS OF HUSBANDRY

Each year Jack and his labourers brought in fine harvests of beans.

Each year First Suit arrived with his ever better-dressed and more prosperous looking entourage.

Each year they left Jack with enough of his year's bean harvest for subsistence and took the rest.

Each year Jack read in the Financial Press and on the Web that his pile of invested beans had grown on an epic scale.

But he never returned to the trailer – and neither did his neighbours who were investing as wisely and cautiously as was Jack.

CLOUDS ON THE HORIZON

And then one year the rains failed and the sun stayed stubbornly behind clouds right up till harvest time. The harvest would not fail altogether. But bean yield was poor. So too was corn yield. Cabbages were sparse. Fat cows grew thin. Disaster loomed.

Villagers were laid off. Crime was up. Politicians blamed each other. The Mayor lost his first election in 20 years to a coalition of fanatical reactionaries and liberals. The Starbucks was on the brink of closure.

THE STORM

And in the autumn sure as eggs is eggs (though not many eggs that year) up rolled the caravan on schedule.

"Hi" said Jack to the Suit. "Gotta problem."

"The harvest is a real dog. So I will just take my dividend and you can give me back a few of that now-vast pile of my invested beans".

"Ah" said First Suit. "We got us a problem too."

"No beans".

Now we should not conclude from the image of Jack that we have from this little history that Jack is a simpleton. Nor should we conclude that Jack is easily pushed around.

Jack had indeed noticed that the Suit was leaving with him each year the very beans he had just harvested. But the honest smile of the Suit and his compadres, the reliability of that which one reads in the Wall Street Journal and the Financial Times (confirmed by real time data gleaned from the Internet) and the size and quality of the bus and the trailer, which were regularly and expensively upgraded and renovated, had reassured Jack that his invested beans, if not in Fort Knox and protected by the Federal Government, did at least exist.

But it appeared now from what the Suit was saying that this was not the case.

"Could you explain?" asked Jack politely.

"Well" said the Suit. "We don't exactly understand ourselves."

"We sold our own service fee beans– the best of the beans we took from your investment pile - for cash. You will be happy to hear that we are now very rich indeed".

"But as to the rest of the beans – yours for example - the beans exist in theory. They exist on paper. They exist fiscally. They exist in our computers and in those of the Inland Revenue. They just don't exist in reality."

"We do have a real stock of objects –think of them as hybrids, or derivatives. There are lots of bits of beans all mixed up with other objects or stuck to them in the most ingenious and creative form. They undoubtedly have some use for somebody and could one day turn out to be negotiable instruments. But, alas they are not coffee beans and could not be used to make coffee".

Jack who was a paid up member of the NRA went quietly into the house to fetch his trusty shotgun.

On emerging from the porch, however, he found lined up outside the house a row of Suits (whose apparel he now noticed was of extremely expensive cloth cut to exquisite shape by obviously gifted and expensive tailors).

In front of the Suits was a row of equally smartly dressed gentlemen each with a large badge bearing the magic words "Attorney-at-Law". And in front of these fellows was another row of burly folk (maybe the word gentlemen does not now apply) in uniform and toting what seemed to be sub machine guns. Their badges signalled the word "Security" and Jack surmised that the security of which they were talking was not his.

He felt it only reasonable to let them depart in peace and so he did.

Jack was left on the porch of his farm with no capital, no income, no money for seed, no money for harvesters' pay and a very gloomy future.

He had some plants with ripe berries yet unharvested – just enough for the family's coffee and that of his neighbours. He had a few to sell. He even had some for Starbucks.

Just as well the Suits didn't know. They probably would have taken that at gunpoint. They wouldn't have done the harvesting work in the fields of course. But a few villagers at the point of a Kalashnikov would have done the job with enthusiasm.

Jack sat on his porch.

He called to his wife and children.

He wept.

He reached for his father's diary.

And started to read.

DO NOT MISS

JACK AND THE BEANCOUNTERS **PART II.**

"ASCENT TO THE LIGHT".

JACK AND THE BEANCOUNTERS

A 21ST CENTURY FABLE

PART II - ASCENT INTO THE LIGHT

THE DARKEST HOUR

With his family seated around him on the porch of their home, Jack read aloud the words of his father – those words to be read "when the bad times come around".

They sure had come around now.

The script stared at Jack as Jack stared at the script.

19 words. No more, no less.

"WHEN THE GOING GETS TOUGH, THE TOUGH GET GOING".

He read it aloud twice.

It was, of course, his far less taciturn wife who broke the silence.

"Jack" she said. "Did you think making money was going to be that easy? Did you really believe those snake oil salesmen? Did you really convince yourself that all there is to life is dressing up in a cute suit, counting beans and cutting them into fancy shapes so as you can glue them back together - and lo there's twice as many as there were before."

"What about the work Jack? What about the planting? What about the watering, the hoeing, the ploughing? What about the pruning, the grafting, the fertilising? What about the fencing to keep the pests out?

"And what about the picking of each bean only when it's ripe for the picking? And the carrying to the storage? And the sacking? And the roasting?"

"And what about the selling? And then the delivery?"

"And how about the going around the customers after the sale to find out what they liked about the beans and what they didn't? And then the seeding to make them better beans the next year?"

"Is all that easy? Or maybe all that work is just plain unnecessary?"

"Is that what the snake oil men told you? Just hand me over your beans and I will give you an income and double your money each year? Is that what you really believed?"

Now Jack adored his lovely lady wife, the fine mother to his fine children and his companion on life's harsh and demanding highway.

But he was not about to be branded even by his beloved wife as an unimaginative moron who had been effortlessly gulled into throwing away the fruit of his and his family's labour without even the bare minimum of mental effort.

Furthermore, like so many devoted husbands throughout history, he felt deeply wounded at being held solely responsible for decisions which had been made jointly and severally by both partners following open and amiable debate over the merits and demerits of the Suit's proposal.

So, with mild impatience and somewhat reduced affection he snarled:

"So if you were so damned smart, why the hell didn't you say something at the time, my beloved?"

There then ensued one of those marital dialogues which are best left unrecorded but which are so key to restoring domestic harmony and the spirit of mutual collaboration in all the best households – when they do not end up in the divorce courts that is.

On this occasion, of course, there emerged a deeper understanding of the roles to be played by the participants and that aura of optimism which can only hover over the household of the most devoted couples.

"It is of course all very easy for the old goat to scrawl self evident truisms."

"'When the going gets tough the tough get going!' Ha!"

Jack showed a measure of most un-filial scorn.

"But how the hell am I supposed to be tough when I have pretty much nothing to get going with? It's all gone. Even the goddamn bean counters have squandered their pile of my beans on booze, travel, executive jets, hookers, gambling and unreachable pension funds domiciled in sand flea infested Caribbean Islands."

THE TOUGH GET GOING

His wife touched his shoulder tenderly and came out with those words of encouragement which can only flow from the heart of the most devoted of wives when they have finally heard enough whingeing from their life's companion.

"Jack" she said. "Jack! You can do it. You really can".

Of course what she really meant was "I can do it. I really can."

And so she did.

"Jack" she said. It is time for us to organise this business. Time to take stock. Time to plan. Time to organise. Time…" (she smiled) ".. to get going!"

"First the current situation. Indeed we have no savings. We have no capital. We have no money for wages and no money for seed."

"But we have a lot of beans on a lot of plants. We have neighbours with corn in the field, cows to fatten and cabbages to lift. We have villagers to work. We have a Starbucks in which to relax after a hard day's toil."

"And we have our brains, unlimited access to the Internet and all the accumulated knowledge of the human race - courtesy of Google. What more do we need?"

She answered her own question (as strong ladies are inclined to do) before Jack could interject.

"Nothing, Jack. We need nothing more."

"Now what do we have to do, who does what and how do we do it?"

"We have to harvest those beans. We have to sell them. And we have to make a profit so we can start to build up our capital, keep on growing and saving each year. Then, Jack we can finally retire, go on several cruises and leave a healthy farm for the kids to build their lives around. And we are going to show the neighbours and the villagers just how it can be done."

"Now the tasks and the roles we are to play."

"You, Jack, will be our Chairman and Managing Director – of course. You will be in charge. You will as always be the boss!"

"You will also be our Director of Operations and Production, Research and Development and Quality

Control. You will be in charge of harvesting the beans, of planting new ones and of tending them as they grow for next year's harvest."

"I, Jack will adopt a more humble role. I will be your Marketing Director, your Sales Director and your Chief Brand Officer. My job will be to sell the beans you produce and to make as much money out of them as we can."

"We will not have a Finance Director, Jack. Our beans will be counted by all of us, they will be priced by me based on what the market will bear and you will make sure we grow them economically. No Bean Counter will work for this restructured company. Never."

"Our Company is hereby named 'Jack's Coffee Corporation'".

"Our slogan will be 'If it's not Jack's Coffee it isn't coffee'".

"We shall prevail".

And so they went to work.

BUSINESS RECOVERY PLAN STAGE 1

In a short space of time the bean harvest was done.

The villagers were not happy to work from sunup to sunset for no cash.

But they had no other work. And enough coffee for their basic caffeine needs for a year sufficed to staunch their grumbling.

Following similar conversations on the neighbouring farms identical solutions were found to identical dilemmas. From now on the reader may assume that what is happening to Jack, his wife and his farm is being replicated on every farm in the county. Such is the benefit of 21st century communications technology.

BUSINESS RECOVERY PLAN STAGE 2

MINUTES OF THE FIRST MEETING OF THE BOARD OF JACK'S COFFEE CORPORATION PLC (INC, SL, SA, GMBH).

"Now Jack" said his wife "please provide a detailed breakdown of our inventory."

Jack cleared his throat.

"We have 10,000 coffee beans following the allocation of beans as wages for the villagers. And I would like to move that the Board express its gratitude to the workforce for a fine job done."

"I would further like to put forward a motion of disapproval and censure in the matter of the Suits and their reprehensible - indeed criminal behaviour - ….."

His wife and recently appointed Marketing Director and Chief Brand Officer interrupted brusquely (and in Jack's opinion quite rudely).

"Ok, Mr Chairman, ok. Cut the crap. Let's get on with some real business. That is the kind of rubbish the Suits do at their Board Meetings. We are here to make an honest buck Jack."

"That inventory isn't worth - if I may jest a moment - a hill of beans".

"Please go away and rework the inventory to give us some useful breakdown. For example sort the stock by size, by colour, by origin, and by any other breakdown that occurs to your somewhat limited brain (Jack was quite hurt by that sharp - albeit true -barb) "I want to know how many big beans we have, how many small and how many of medium size."

"I want to know how many light coloured and how many dark are. I want to know which ones were grown on the hills and how many in the valleys and how many on the flat. I want to know how many are suited for immediate roasting and how many can wait."

"I want to know, in other words, something I can work with."10.000 beans" tells me nothing. It's just a problem. We need solutions."

The Board meeting was adjourned – not without some acidity in the air – but adjourned nonetheless while Jack stumped off to do some serious bean sorting.

BUSINESS RECOVERY PLAN STAGE 3

MINUTES OF THE SECOND MEETING OF THE BOARD OF JACK'S COFFEE CORPORATION PLC (INC, SL, SA, GMBH).

"Meeting comes to order."

Jack's wife somehow seemed to have moved to the head of the table and was acting every bit like a Chairman.

But Jack knew he was really in charge and so decided to humour his adored – not to mention highly respected, if not feared – lady.

Jack once again pondered the immortal words of the Duke of Wellington to his ADC as he reviewed his troops marching to the Field of Waterloo:

"They may not frighten the French, Sir, but by God they frighten me."

"Jack" demanded his wife "please give us your revised inventory – with breakdowns"

"Extra large beans 2000. Large beans 2000. Medium beans 4000. Small beans 2000."

"Dark beans 5000. Light coloured beans 5000"

"Hillside beans 5000. Plains beans 2500. Valley beans 2500"

"Rain watered beans 6000. Beans watered by irrigation from the spring fed stream 4000"

"Beans that in my judgement would benefit from roasting now 5000. Beans that can wait and assume more flavour with age 5000"

"Well done, Jack. Well done".

Jack blushed at the unwonted praise and felt motivated to do better.

"Now Jack for the marketing plan I have prepared"

"First we are going to roast all our beans ourselves. We will add value. Roasted beans fetch a higher price. We add value by roasting. Ordinary consumers don't have much in the way of roasting facilities. We roast better and more conveniently. All Jack's coffee will be roasted."

"Secondly, we will grind half the beans and they will be sold as packs of freshly ground beans. The other half will be sold as un-ground beans so that the consumer who likes to grind their own can have coffee ground just seconds before brewing – you cant get fresher than that – and these un-ground, natural beans will be sold to our consumers as the perfect bean for grinding yourself."

"We will offer Jack's coffee to suit all the different tastes, requirements, needs and dreams of our consumers".

"_Hand selected small beans_ for more concentrated flavour. _Big beans_ for big flavour."

"_Spring watered beans_ for pure taste. _Rain watered beans_ for natural organic taste."

"_Mountain beans_" (Jack protested mildly at this inflation of their modest hillside to mountain status, but was rightly brushed aside) "for grandeur and depth of flavour. _Plains beans_ for sturdy reliability."

"_Early roasted beans_ for the fashion conscious early adopter. _Late roasted beans_ for the cautious, discerning, deep thinker."

"And all will command a premium price over _Jack's Basic Beans_ – of which happily for our profitability there will be only a small volume of production available for the un-discerning consumer- of whom we have only one I recall – the recently ejected Mayor".

"Finally, Jack, as Director of Operations and Production, Research and Development and Quality Control, you will be responsible for ensuring a steady flow of _Hand selected small beans_, _Big beans_, _Spring watered beans, Rain watered beans,_ Mountain _beans_, _Plains beans_, _Early roasted beans_, and even _Jack's Basic Beans_ in the precise ratios that I prescribe, based on the needs, preferences and desires of our customers - which I will identify.

Jack, recognising some imminent dilution of his status as Boss, not to mention his self esteem as Director of

Operations and Production, Research and Development and Quality Control, reasserted himself at this point. He requested a full cost, price and profit analysis for each of the variant brand extensions listed by his wife, who was now positively glowing with a (he thought extremely attractive, if not positively erotic) flush of conceptual creativity.

The Chairman – momentarily overcoming his own sudden creative urge – pronounced, with that wisdom and foresight that only the Chairman can bring to the Boardroom table:

"If we sell all our beans at these premium prices we will indeed have a surplus for working capital, investment and eventually retirement with a slew of cruises" he said admiringly.

"What is more if the neighbours apply the same approach to their corn, livestock and cabbages as we do to our beans, they too can come on the cruises with us."

THE SUN SHINES ON THE RIGHTEOUS

And so it came to pass.

The bean business flourished and made lots and lots of money with each brand extension a successful profit centre.

The neighbours prospered. The villagers went back to work. The Mayor was re-elected. Starbucks added a drive through. Jack and his wife retired. And to this day they are cruising the world with their neighbours - all living happily ever after.

The Suits are in jail (or should be).

The Consumer is Queen (and occasionally King) of coffee, corn, cabbages, livestock derivatives and every imaginable consumer product and service.

Marketing Rules the Waves and the Land.

Resistance is Futile.

©Marketingcompass.org
Cambridge January 2012

www.ingramcontent.com/pod-product-compliance
Lightning Source LLC
Chambersburg PA
CBHW071554170526
45166CB00004B/1671